AF439588

Contents

Introduction

Having just made the life-changing decision to up-sticks and move away from Bedfordshire, giving up a Victorian family home and secure(ish) job for a rented modern-built boxy house and the joys of job-hunting, albeit in a beautiful part of the country, I decided to re-visit something that had once been very important in my life but which I had dropped during the 'making a family' events of the past few years.

It was a gloriously hot summer's day, and I had decided to make a new set of runes to replace the ones that had resided, largely unused, in their leather pouch for the past five or so years. I had found a lovely piece of yew from a nearby wood and was sanding the cut discs smooth. My mind wandered back a decade or more to the time when Paul and I were close friends at college. We had shared an interest in the esoteric and had developed our knowledge of the runes together, sharing experiences and trips to Avebury and Glastonbury and generally having a pretty good time. We had drifted apart, I moved to Bedfordshire, he to Devon.

As I sat in the warm afternoon sun I thought "I wonder what Paul's up to?", and thought nothing more of him. I finished sanding and marking the set, popped them into the bag, burnt the old set and, the following day, drove to Avebury.

Walking up the street from the car park towards the pub I heard the sound of music and bells – Morris dancing was being perpetrated. I instantly recognised the tall, long-haired chap throwing himself around with gusto despite the fact that I hadn't seen him for years. When the dance finished I tapped him on the shoulder. He turned, his jaw dropped and he hugged me.

After he let me go he looked straight into my eyes and said "What the hell are you doing here?". I showed him my runes.

His response was immediate. "This is so weird. I took my runes down from the top of the cupboard yesterday afternoon for the first time in years and thought "I wonder what Keith's doing", and here you are."

I told him then about my own thoughts. We worked out that they had happened simultaneously.

All my life I have been searching for something spiritual. I have looked at religion, new age beliefs, Buddhism, shamanism and witchcraft and found nothing that convinces me there is anything out there. I am an atheist, and seem to become more so the older I get. I have no time for the rigmarole and ritual framework of mainstream religion. I want to see something real, that doesn't rely on pre-conditioning or acceptance of what others tell me is the truth.

When I was going through my formative years, Chinese and Celtic mysticism were really coming to the fore. I tried looking at both, but the Chinese was too far removed from the society in which I had been raised and relied on the acceptance of knowledge that was alien to my western culture while the Celtic ideas all seemed rather mismatched and fluffy. They bore no real relation to the Celts that the Romans had written about and seemed to introduce ideas that cannot have been real to the people they were supposed to represent – a people that never developed a written language. Where were these ideas coming from? Where were the Celtic Shaman Cards from? Where did the concepts behind the Celtic Tree Alphabet come from? The answer, of course, is that they are, in large part, made up – an amalgam of different ideas and spirituality from various pagan cultures that actually have nothing to do with the Celts.

This time also saw the rise of the 'new-age', with all the nonsense and pseudo-science that entailed. It was this, more than anything else, that disillusioned me. However, at around the same time – 1983 – I bought Ralph Blum's "Book of runes" and fell in love.

Which just goes to show that love is blind.

Blum's book was just as bad as the Celtic and new-age stuff I hated. So, for years I have searched and searched for something that would explain how I felt, that would enable me to look at my life and see a depth and meaning that didn't rely on ritual or having to compromise my own logic and acceptance of the scientific. Most importantly I wanted something that would ground me, that would really give me a sense of belonging to this beautiful country that didn't involve nationalism, flag-waving or football. Something that was Western, that was real, that had a degree of integrity, that wasn't a sop to the gullible and that made me think.

What I didn't realise was that I had already found it. I just had to understand it.

Wyrd is...

I first encountered the concept of wyrd about twenty years ago, thanks to a little book called "The Book of Runes" by Ralph Blum. It barely mentioned it, just saying that the 'blank' rune (more on which later) was symbolic of it and that it stood for unknowable fate. The word was nicely 'strange', it spoke of something deeper without actually requiring any research and it meant that any time the 'blank' rune came up I could sit back and look knowingly around while thinking to myself "damn, that's impossible to interpret".

A little while later I came across another book entitled "The Way of Wyrd" by Dr. Brian Bates. This book, a novel based around Anglo-Saxon pagan beliefs, was what really started me down the path I am still weaving along so many years later. In this book, a young Christian scribe is called on by his Abbot to journey through Mercia in order to understand the pagan beliefs of the locals. He is guided by Wulf, a sorcerer and shaman. The book is entertaining and informative and I highly recommend you reading it – after finishing this one.

What Bates did was to place wyrd (and the runes for that matter) in a living, vibrant world where they were seen as part of both the mundane and spiritual. However, there is still a problem, as he acknowledges:-

Maybe I should start again...

Wyrd is...again

Having picked up on the idea that wyrd is an important concept, albeit one that is difficult to describe, I started looking for contemporary sources to see what the people who really lived with it felt. The best known example of Anglo-Saxon poetry is Beowulf – the epic story of a hero's various struggles written sometime between 650 and 1000 AD. The first real example of the language that became known as Englisc (the sound of the letters 'sc' being pronounced as the modern 'sh'), it contains the following line:-

Which neatly sums up Beowulf's rather fatalistic approach to an upcoming battle. In the context of the poem this line is not to be seen as a shrug, a fancy way of saying "hey ho – what will be will be", but more as an acknowledgement that certain events will unfold as they will regardless of the preparation one is able to put into them. Beowulf knows that there is a good chance he will die in the struggle, but also that there is a good chance he will prevail. Until the fight concludes these outcomes are in flux.

Later, when Beowulf comes up against the dragon, he realises that this time he is not going to win:-

> *"And for the first time in his life that famous prince fought with fate against him, with glory denied him"*

A quick perusal of other sources reveals the following statements:-

> *"Wyrd's shaping changes the world under heaven."*

> *"A weary mood won't withstand wyrd, nor may the troubled mind find help."*

This is beginning to help. We are getting the idea that wyrd is separate from religion, that it is an active force for change but that it is not something that can be called upon to get us out of trouble. One thing is certain though. Looking at these statements, the idea that wyrd is simply 'fate' is far too simplistic.

In order to get the idea across to Brand, the scribe in The Way of Wyrd, Wulf describes the Norse entities known as the Norns. These figures, the maiden, mother and crone, the archetypal three witches in Macbeth, representative of all stages of life, sit at the roots of the tree which separates heaven and the underworld from the Earth, working at a loom on which the lives of men are spun. The vertical threads represent the path of a person's life, while the horizontal lines are the events that happen during that life. The shape of the weave is constantly shifting and changing as the Norns break threads or introduce new ones as people are born and die. While this view is beautifully poetic, it raises a question, particularly in light of the Anglo-Saxon quotes above. Given that wyrd is separate from God and that it seems to have no personality, how can it be that it is controlled, almost on a whim, by beings outside the 'real' world? Something there doesn't seem to fit with the way wyrd was experienced by the English.

It may be that a better understanding of the Anglo-Saxon world could help.

Following the dissolving of the Roman Empire, Britain slowly devolved into a set of small Romano-British kingdoms. In the years that followed, the most eastern of these, situated in Kent, Norfolk, Suffolk and Sussex, were subjected to raids from people hailing from what would become Germany. These people settled and quickly spread, forcing the indigenous people to the north and west. The invading people brought their own beliefs and gods and quickly displaced the indigenous tribes.

In around 500AD, Christianuty arrived, and spread. By around 800AD, Christianity had established itself as the predominant religion across much of England. Despite this the belief in and acceptance of wyrd continued, separate from religion as evidenced by the following from beautiful poem, The Wanderer :-

"Wyrd is greater and God is mightier than any man's thought".

What seems to be happening is that the Christian God simply replaces the old pagan Gods, with wyrd still acting on a different level entirely. It is almost as if God provides the personality behind existence while wyrd provides the structure. This idea is further enhanced by the translation of the Gospel according to John which begins with the beautiful phrase "in the beginning was the word, and the word was with God".

This Gospel was translated into Old English (Anglo-Saxon) by St. Bede in 735 AD. This opening line has been the subject of much discussion among Christians, even now there are whole sites on the internet dedicated to attempts to understand what Bede was trying to say. Being Anglo-Saxon Bede would have grown up fully conversant with the ideas and concepts behind wyrd – it would have been as much a part of his make-up as his Christianity undoubtedly was later in his life. That Bede understood wyrd is borne out by the fact that the original translation sees "word" written as "wyrd", and suddenly the phrase makes complete sense.

However, the idea that God is only part of the picture is not politically viable, particularly when the early Christian church spent so much time changing pagan beliefs and morals. This is not the place for a detailed exposition of the strangeness of early Christian thinking, but I can't help thinking that if the Anglo-Saxon version with its separation of personality and power had been kept we may not have seen a lot of the bloodshed and pain that we did.

Pagan eyes saw a vastly different world from the one we see now. Nowadays we live in a world where science has answered many of the questions and solved many of the problems that would have exercised our forefather's minds. Health and lifespan are vastly improved, although the average Anglo-Saxon could, barring violence, hope to live well into his sixties. We have an understanding of the universe that they couldn't even guess at – we know the scope and age of the vastness around us; we know how we came to be here, we understand our place in the universe on a very physical level. We even have a good idea of how the fundamental building blocks of our matter work (more of which in the next chapter). All of this was not only unknown to the Anglo-Saxons, it was unknowable. Their world was immediate. They had to live without planning and forethought – at least on the scale we are able to do now. A good harvest meant an easy winter, a poor summer meant death.

Early English society was feudal, with a strict hierarchical class-structure. The average person simply did not have the opportunities offered him by modern society. Disease was a very real threat. The current media panic over swine 'flu shows how far removed we have become from understanding what disease can really do to society. For the Anglo-Saxon 'flu could be a very real threat, but it was but one of a myriad of infections that could make life interesting, and short, for vast numbers of the population. Plague, smallpox and cholera (although this was rarer – cholera thrives in squalid conditions where drinking water is easily contaminated by faecal matter, hence the problems it caused in Victorian London) were all available for the discerning patient to catch.

Theirs was a violent society. Skirmishes between tribes were commonplace, and the Vikings were a continual thorn in the side for hundreds of years. Battlefield prowess was central to the English, and boasting of victories provided entertainment. To modern sensibilities they were vicious, arrogant bullies.

They were also, of course, capable of sublime poetry, exquisite metalwork and detailed art, which helps to mollify their rough appearance.

Anglo-Saxon life was harsh, beautiful, vicious, sublime and immediate and there was no line drawn between the mundane and the spiritual. Everything had a soul, this was self-evident for the soul breathed out the form, without soul nothing can exist. The soul was not some aspect of spirit that was special or inaccessible, it was integral to the survival of the individual. Spirits pervaded everyday life, from elves that soured milk to the great spirits of the woods and the land. Wrapped around all of this was wyrd.

To the early English, wyrd was all-pervasive. It simultaneously controlled and was controlled by life. Nothing could happen without it, but it provided no guidance of itself. To the sorceror it was the very stuff of life, a tool that he (or she) could use but never control.

I am not one for the "lost ancient knowledge" way of thinking. The idea that ancient civilisations had access to technologies that have disappeared leaving no trace is evidentially woolly. However, that they had access to different ways of thinking is obvious. Some of these are, without doubt, best left for dead, but many are worthy of re-considering.

Wyrd is certainly one of these.

Having had my little rant I should point out that what follows is largely conjecture. As we have seen, written accounts of wyrd are scant, and I have had to piece together thoughts and phrases from various sources to try and make sense of a world view that is somewhat different to my original, Twentieth-Century one. The following chapters range happily from quantum mechanics to psychology, they take biology, geology and evolution in their stride and ramble through ideas on spirituality and folklore before alighting on the runes – all in an effort to describe something that is largely indescribable. Hopefully the result is entertaining. I would be happy to think that it may also be a cause for thought.

The Ball of String Theory

This chapter is going to be a bit of a roller-coaster, I'm afraid. It will introduce some concepts that require a degree of imagination to grasp and will spend some time looking at other ideas that will either help to illustrate what I am trying to get across, or will simply serve to confuse the issues. I hope they do the former, but the latter is certainly a possibility. Now that we have an idea of wyrd from an historical perspective we need to start moving forward. However, in order to move forward it is sometimes necessary to go backwards. In this instance we are going back a little way – to around 1900 – where we shall meet some extraordinary thinkers who changed the way the universe was understood to work.

Prior to this time the universe worked according to some pretty simple rules – primarily those developed by Isaac Newton and published in deliberately confused fashion in 1687. Newton was, without doubt, a genius of the highest order. He was a prolific thinker and produced over the course of his life an amount of work that would happily fill the lives, and ensure the lasting fame, of ten lesser people. Among his astonishing ideas lay the Laws of Motion, the Laws of Conservation of Energy, the invention of the reflecting telescope, the concept that white light is made of different colours, the mathematical description of the way planets move, the invention of a whole new branch of maths (along with Gottfried Leibniz) called calculus and he was deemed more influential on the history of science than Albert Einstein in a survey conducted by the Royal Society in 2005.

In 1687 he published his great work, the Philosophiæ Naturalis Principia Mathematica, known more simply as the Principia. Its three books contained the backbone of what came to be known as physics and the mathematics contained within are still used to calculate things like the trajectories of space flights today. As an interesting aside it was nearly never published at all. The usual route was for new scientific works to be published by the Royal Society in London, but the Society had spent all its money that year on a book detailing the history of fish. It was only because another great man, Edmund Halley (who had approached Newton to develop a method of calculating the orbital path of a planet as a means of settling a bet), stumped up the cash that it ever saw the light of day. Newton was too much of a snob to fund the publication himself.

The Principia quickly asserted itself as a best seller, despite the third volume which was made deliberately difficult to understand by Newton so that only those of a high enough social standing (and therefore intelligence) could grasp its importance. The History of Fishes meanwhile, nearly bankrupted the Royal Society.

The impact of the Principia cannot be over-stated and it forms an understanding of the universe that is as true today as it was 300 years ago.

As it turned out, however, it was not quite true enough. In 1915 a small paper was published that changed the universe. Running to an impressive five pages and coming from a young German-born man who had spent his formative years working in a Swiss patent office. It was called the Theory of General Relativity and it fundamentally changed the way the universe was perceived.

One of the problems in a Newtonian universe is that time doesn't get a look in. In fact, according to Newton's maths, time is irrelevant. It can run in any direction and it will make no difference to the calculations. While this actually doesn't matter for the most part it is obviously a bit of a poser. Einstein solved this issue by proposing that time and space are not separate, but are actually different components of the same thing, which he called space/time. This suddenly explains not only the effects of gravity, for example, which Newton had so famously worked on, but why gravity exists at all. In the Einsteinian universe gravity is the product of mass. Massive objects warp space/time much as a rubber sheet is stretched by heavy balls placed upon it.

Whilst both these men produced work that elegantly described the workings of the universe on a large scale, when things get very small both models begin to fall apart.
As technology improved scientists began to look closely at the universe on an atomic scale and what they found simply made no sense. Not only did they not make sense, they didn't make sense on a quite spectacular scale.

This new branch of physics was dubbed Quantum Mechanics, and Einstein hated it. The effects that were being observed at the atomic level were so strange, so different from what his theories predicted that he spent the last few years of his life trying desperately to come up with a theory that would bring the atomic universe into line with the visible one.

He failed.

Indeed he is recorded as saying "Marvellous, what ideas the young people have these days. But I don't believe a word of it". He was not alone, and many of those scientists at the heart of the new physics were equally appalled at what was being shown. Indeed, the Nobel Prize-winning physicist Niels Bohr, whose work was fundamental to understanding the structure of atoms, has said "those who are not shocked when they first come across quantum theory cannot possibly have understood it."

So, what makes this line of physics so strange?

Do you remember the drawings of atoms you saw in school text books? You know the ones I mean – the ones that look like a miniature solar system with the nucleus sitting nicely in the centre and little ball-shaped electrons whizzing around on their own discreet orbits? Well, it turns out that they are about as inaccurate as it is possible for a diagram to be. The scale is wrong for a start. Let's look at a Hydrogen atom – this is the simplest thing to start with. One proton in the nucleus (don't worry about the terminology, we won't need to go into any great detail) and one electron orbiting it. Easy to draw and it fits nicely on a page.

Except...

If you were to draw it on a computer to scale with the smallest thing a computer can display – a pixel – representing the smallest part of the atom, the electron, the proton in the nucleus would be 1000 pixels across. Noticeably bigger than the electron but able to fit comfortably on the screen. The distance between the proton and the orbiting electron would be, wait for it, eleven miles. That probably bears repeating. Eleven miles. The space in between is occupied by nothing. Really nothing. And the electron is not a little ball. It is (and this is where it all begins to get odd) nothing more than the possibility of an electrical charge, so it should be represented by a sort of fuzzy cloud. In more complex atoms the electrons occupy multiple orbits, similar to the way the planets occupy distinct positions around the sun.

However, unlike planets, the electrons can sometimes change their orbits, shifting from one to another but without passing through the intervening space. It would be like you deciding to visit your aunt and appearing instantly in her living room. It is, in effect, teleportation. In order for this to happen they travel faster than the speed of light, something which is, according to Einstein's most famous equation (you know the one; $E=MC2$), impossible.

As the electrons are simply fuzzy clouds of possibility this also means that you have never actually touched anything. When you sit on a chair or pick up an apple the electrons from your respective atoms repel each other, meaning that you are actually separated from the chair or apple by the distance between electrons. It's pretty small, admittedly, but it is there. All you have ever touched is electrons. In fact, going a little further, you don't actually exist. Most of the space in the atoms that construct you is, as we saw earlier, completely empty. You are, in a very real sense, greater than the sum of your parts, as the parts themselves are, to all intents and purposes, nothing.

Things get even more strange when we go to the sub-atomic level and start looking at particles – the things that make atoms. At this scale, the strangeness gets, well, stranger. Some sub-atomic particles have a property known as spin.

This is effectively exactly what it says – they can rotate around their central axis. Being the odd things they are they don't always rotate the way one would expect, sometimes requiring one-and-a-half or even two spins to get them the right way 'up' again. What is really odd about some of them is that they operate in pairs. When one spins its opposite number spins as well, in exactly the same way - simultaneously. The odd part is that this reaction occurs wherever in the universe they happen to be. So, if one spins, the other will spin in sympathy even if they are separated by hundreds of light years of space. There is some property connecting these particles that causes these effects completely regardless of distance.

The point of this excursion into the foggy realms of quantum mechanics is to highlight a fundamental aspect of wyrd. The traditional view of wyrd is that of cloth on a loom with the vertical strands representing the progress of your life and the horizontal threads being events that happen to you. While this view works quite well on a personal level it fails, much as Newton's maths fail, when applied to a different scale. It is far too small and neat.

What follows is a thought experiment, but one that you are more than welcome to try in reality should you wish. Actually, I would love it if you did and sent me photographs of the resulting confusion.

The next time you leave the house take with you many infinitely long balls of string. I realise that to do this in reality would be tricky. Anyway, to start, tie one end of a ball of string to the door and pay it out as you go about your business. When you are required to make your first choice – turning at a junction, deciding when to cross a road, doing that little dance that people do when they approach each other and can't decide which side to pass on – cut the string to your house and tie another ball to the end, making a knot. Each time you make subsequent decisions do the same thing.

When you meet someone and interact with them, however briefly, give them a ball of string and tie one end to the string that leads from that point back to your house. You won't need to worry about giving them instructions – they'll know exactly what to do.

As you go through your day the web of string attached to you will, of course, become ever more complex as it winds around your life, splitting off here and there to other people's lives and theirs, in turn, splitting off to others. Looking back you will be able to see every decision you have made, every person you have dealt with up to that point represented by knots and joints in your web of string.

Now, this analogy is fine as far as it goes. It does have some limitations, of course. Primary among these is the fact that no-one would be able to move after a couple of minutes, and a car coming along would wreak havoc with people pinging around like bouncy balls. So – now that you have the idea in your mind, replace the string with blue light. It is far prettier after all and much less likely to get tangled. It also allows us to operate in time.

Re-trace your path from your door, this time leaving a thick line of light behind you. When you reach the first knot where you made a decision replace the knot with the faint traceries of every other decision you could have taken trailing off and fading away from that point. When you reach the first intersection where you met someone see how thick or thin their line is. If it is someone you have never met before it will probably be fading, if it is a friend the line will be thick. Retrace your entire day this way, replacing the string with light, the knots with choices.

Now pull back, allow yourself to float above the world and see your web from above. See how it is intertwined with those of the people you meet, see the faint lines of decisions you did not take fade the further from your main line they go. Now use your mind to imagine this happening since the day you were born.

Onto this enormous vision we need to add another dimension. We need it to be able to look forwards in time as well. As you journey through your day see how the line actually stretches before you, fainter than the line you leave, but definitely there. There are knots in front of you, but the choices emanating from these knots do not fade, they are as strong as the rest of the future-line, fanning out before you in an infinitely complex pattern, only fading and disappearing as you reach a knot and choose a path to follow. This future-web is constantly shifting and changing as more choices appear depending on the actions you take.

This is your wyrd.

Let's go back to the string version for a while. Ignore all the technical issues about weight, cars and rogue cats swinging from it and just take some time to see the complexity of the web around you. Then reach down and gently twang a strand. A ripple of movement will spread along the string, vibrating the whole web as it passes the knots and joints. With a string version this transmission is limited to the speed of a ripple, something around walking speed; it will also fade the further it goes from the point of origin.

If we switch back to the glowing-light version these limitations are not so important. This time, as you pluck a strand, you might see slow ripples spreading along it that suddenly accelerate when they reach a knot, streaking along the line to reach their target almost instantly. You may have noticed that those people closest to you sometimes pick up on your moods before you speak to them – this is (as far as I am concerned anyway) the reason why. Sometimes the information travelling along the strands of wyrd manages to reach its destination at the same time as it was propagated – in a similar manner to particles reacting to each other across the universe (see, there was a reason for going through all that physics earlier).

Try and keep this visual analogy with you as we move on – it will hopefully help with some of the concepts coming up. This is going to be a demanding ride, but the next chapter settles down a bit, so put the kettle on and look forward to a coffee. So far we have looked at wyrd as a passive product of the choices we make and the people we meet. While this is a good start it is only a part of the whole picture.
I'm afraid that we will have to saunter back into the heady world of quantum theory for a while in order to illustrate an aspect of wyrd that seems at first thought completely counter - intuitive.

So, back to 1935 and a correspondence between Albert Einstein and another of the great thinkers of the time, an Austrian named Erwin Schrodinger. Schrodinger was a theoretical physicist who had won a Nobel Prize two years earlier for his development of an equation that became as central to quantum mechanics as Newton's Laws are to standard mechanics. In an effort to describe to Einstein the

fundamental strangeness of things at the sub-atomic level he
came up with an idea that most people have heard of even if
the importance of it is not generally appreciated.
The problem that he was trying to describe is based on
the idea that, in quantum physics, you can know either the
position of a particle or its direction of travel, but you cannot
know both at the same time. I'm not going to embark on an
explanation at this time, you'll have to take it from me that
this is the case. The important part was that he attempted to
explain this to Einstein by using an allegory that suits us well at
this point.

Take a cat. Any cat will do as long as it is alive. Place this
cat into a box that prevents you seeing what the cat is doing.
Into the box you also place a glass jar of poison (Schrodinger
uses Hydrocyanic poison, or Hydrogen Cyanide as it is now
known). Attached to the jar is a hammer and a trigger which,
when activated will smash the jar releasing the poison with
predictably unfortunate results for the cat. The trigger is set off
by a Geiger counter which will measure the decay of a small
sample of radioactive material. The amount of material is very
small, such that within the hour duration of the experiment
it may, or may not, release a particle which will trigger the
hammer.

The box is then sealed.

As the event that triggers the hammer falling is completely
random, logic dictates that the cat is both alive and dead at any
given point in time. Only when the lid is lifted and the state of
the cat is revealed is it possible to say with certainty which state
the cat is in. Until that time the cat is simultaneously dead and
alive. The point of this idea is to demonstrate that the act of
observing something (in this instance the vitality of a cat, in
quantum theory the position of a particle) fixes it in space.
Until that observation is made however the actual state of the
particle (or cat) can only be guessed.

Terry Pratchett has added that there is another state the cat can be in which, as a cat owner myself seems to be the most likely for an animal locked in a box whilst being both dead and alive at the same time, and that state is "bloody furious".

Schrodinger's Cat ably demonstrates one of the fundamental aspects of wyrd when looking forward in time. Remember all the possible choices that were visible emanating from the future-knots in the glowing version of our web?

Like the cat they exist in potential only.

When you arrive at a knot there are always choices open to you, but which way you travel is not pre-determined, the choice is entirely down to you. It may well be, of course, that despite many options being available there is only actually one route that is really open to you, but that is as a result of the choices you have made up to that point (along with the choices other people have made that shape your wyrd) coupled with your own views on what those choices will entail. Just as the cat is fixed in a state when the box is opened the future paths will either be made real or dissolve depending upon your action.

When you step back and look at the web of your life the way we have done it should become apparent that any choices available to you at any given point in time are entirely your responsibility. While other people's wyrd will undoubtedly impact upon the shape of yours, and will sometimes change the choices you may make when you come to a knot, the actual choice is yours and yours alone.

Wyrd Landscape

Now that I've whittered on for a while about wyrd on a personal level you'll be pleased to know that the time has come to go outside and stretch our legs. As we have seen the actual references for wyrd are few and far between, and this chapter will take ideas rather beyond what the Anglo-Saxon chroniclers chose to relate. This does not mean that the concepts that follow are wrong, merely that they were not written down.

It is important to remember that wyrd was not an Anglo-Saxon invention. The concept was carried by the Norse as they roamed Western Europe. No doubt they also carried it with them when they went to America. However, it is simply a re-naming of a far older idea – an idea that is found world-wide but that has been forgotten in 'civilised' societies. It is only now being recognised as something that is important and that should be cherished and used to help form political and environmental strategy.

I was brought up in Wiltshire in the south of England. Wiltshire is the home of some of the most impressive examples of Neolithic construction anywhere in the world – Stonehenge and the monuments at Avebury, some twenty miles to the north. These structures dominate the landscape, but dotted around them is a huge array of smaller sites, mainly burial mounds known as barrows but with several smaller stone circles scattered around, many of which pre-date the main monument. West Kennet Long Barrow, for example, sitting on a ridge overlooking Silbury Hill and Avebury dates from 3600 BCE and pre-dates the earliest stages of construction of the main henge by some 400 years. It remained in use for around 1,000 years.

On visiting these sites many people feel a connection with the Earth more profound than is usually felt. Given the length of time these sites have been in existence, the length of time that people lived and died in and around them, each with his or her wyrd interweaving around friends and loved ones and communities coming together for rituals this is hardly surprising. That they are built on a scale that meant an incredible undertaking by entire communities the like of which the modern world simply has no call for also means that, as we stand and look, we are hit with a sense of common purpose that is alien to us.

The other worldliness of sites like Avebury coupled with the fact that the people who built them left no records of their motives for doing so, have meant that multiple hypotheses have been put forward to explain their construction. The most likely seem to be based around ritual celebrations, however, aliens and Merlin have both been implicated in their construction.

One hypothesis which I like very much links Avebury and Stonehenge to rites surrounding death and the afterlife. At Avebury there is a site now called The Sanctuary which was originally connected to the main circle by a long avenue of stones. The Sanctuary was a wooden structure, possibly a large roundhouse. A mile north east of Stonehenge lies Durrington Walls, a massive henge monument bigger even than Avebury. It had a similar structure to the Sanctuary placed just outside the banks. The theory, put forward by Professor Mark Parker Pearson, is that the wooden structures were used for celebrations and rituals associated with the living, while the stone monuments were gateways to the lands of the dead. Processing a body from the Sanctuary to the great circle at Avebury or from Woodhenge at Durrington to Stonehenge via the river Avon would enable it to complete a metaphorical journey from a building that would decay and need replacing to one that would, to all intents and purposes, be everlasting.

These monuments were also, like West Kennet Long Barrow, used for a long period, at least 1,000 years. Such long periods of use, and use that must have been highly emotionally charged, could have enabled these sites to develop a wyrd of their own – a feeling that warped the web of those people using them that would, over time, become associated with them.

What is certain is that the areas around these sites have been occupied for many thousands of years, and that amount of life and interaction is bound to leave its mark.

That these areas are special is backed up by local folklore. Many sites around the British Isles have stories associated with them, including strange experiences, ghosts, moving and uncountable stones, spectral black dogs or entrances to other worlds.

In England alone there are thirty nine sites where standing stones are said to move. They rotate, run round fields or rumble over the countryside to local wells or rivers to drink.

Examples include:-

> The Nine Ladies circle in Derbyshire comes alive at midnight to dance.
>
> The large diamond-shaped stone at the
>
> Beckhampton entrance to Avebury crosses the road at midnight.
>
> The Eagle Stone in Baslow turns itself over at midnight.
>
> The Wishing Stone at Bettiscombe, Dorset trundles down the hill on which it stands on Midsummer eve, to return the following morning.
>
> The stone in the centre of Colwall is said to be turned by the Devil every midnight.

The stone next to the River Usk at Crickhowell leaps into the river once a year.

Two large stones close to the Giant's Grave round barrow in Dorset move when they hear a cockerel crowing in the nearby village of Chesilborne.

The stones at Evenjobb walk to Hindwell Pool to drink every night.

The Long Stone near Minchinhampton in Gloucestershire is supposed to run around its field at midnight.

Many people believe that the Earth has its own energies, that it is of itself, alive. If that is the case then the Earth would have its own wyrd, and that is bound to echo and resonate with ours. Could it be that these stones are placed in areas where the Earth's wyrd is particularly resonant? Or is it that the original purpose of these stones was to serve as gathering points and they have 'remembered' the wyrd produced by the intensity of the gatherings?

This feeds in to many other ideas. The obvious is, of course, ley lines but there are many other concepts worldwide that also link to this.

Ley lines were originally proposed by Alfred Watkins in 1921 in his book "The Old Straight Track". He noticed that archaeological structures tended to line up, even though not directly visible from each other. Watkins' idea was that the country was crisscrossed by a network of ancient track ways and paths, enabling travel to be accomplished relatively easily in the dense forests that covered Britain. Watkins never attributed any mystical or magical significance to these alignments whatsoever. Later writers however, have made some interesting discoveries. In particular Captain Robert Boothby and Reginald A. Smith of the British Museum have used dowsing to uncover a range of underground streams and waterways that coincide with leys. Janet and Colin Bord, in their book "Mysterious Britain" took this idea a little further, maintaining that these streams affect the energy of the people living above them and that many standing stones and stone circles are placed where they are to help control or modify the energy generated by the leys. Given the amount of strange occurrences and folk-stories around these sites it is clear that something odd is happening.

Their hypothesis is that the stories of stones moving or turning are actually folk memories of the Earth energy changing polarity or switching direction, rather than the stones themselves moving and that the stories are linked more with feeling than physicality.

If this is the case, and certain places are more attuned to these energies then our view of wyrd needs to alter slightly. It needs to expand to become something that is simultaneously made by life, and that can influence feelings and emotions.

Many of you, being the discerning people you no doubt are, will recognise this; particularly when applied to ancient sites. However...

I'll come right out now and say it. I have a huge problem with some sites; Glastonbury in particular. While I am in no doubt that it is a site of ancient and powerful belief it has become a Mecca for the strange and disturbing. This is not the place to go into all the things I find distasteful about the New Age circus that has grown up around Glastonbury but one thought keeps nagging at me. How much of the 'specialness' of the place is real and how much is down to the wyrd that so many people who expect it to be special have brought with them? If wyrd can exist in the landscape and can influence thought and emotion what happens when that wyrd is hijacked by those people who should be most attuned to it?

I should point out that I don't mean in any way that this
is intentional, however there has been a steady move away
from anything grounded in reality towards a large dose of
wishful thinking in the New Age literature over recent years.
Glastonbury, with its close association to the Arthurian
mythology should be one place that remains grounded – after
all the legend is anything but fluffy. However, a quick wander
through its streets reveals a bewildering amount of angels,
crystals and Celtic and Native American tat, all of which seem
to treat life as something transient that requires a security
blanket of faith to negotiate peacefully. It's almost as if the
town itself has become a parody of what its occupants wish it
to be. One thing that wyrd, or the land, or those people who
erected standing stones is not is fluffy. The Celts were tough,
as happy to butcher each other as they were to fight Romans,
American Indians fought each-other constantly and like the
Anglo-Saxons closely associated with all that life and death
have to offer. It is only in recent times – the last forty or so
years - that civilisation has allowed us to be removed from
the more savage aspects of life, and this coincides with the
rise of the belief that anyone can be a shaman, that faeries
are little winged people who bring out the best in us and that
spirituality means incense, flowing dresses and a willingness to
see the 'good' in everything. We have lost the land, and with it
the connection to life, red in tooth and claw.

I'm not saying for one minute that this is necessarily a bad
thing, but it would do us good in the Western World to regain
a sense of perspective; a sense that life for most of our history,
and for the majority of people now, is hard and painful. The
change in traditional beliefs away from the capriciousness of
the real world to a cosy, kind, rose-coloured wish-fulfillment
helps divorce actions from consequences.

A recent episode of a cookery and travel programme
starring cheeky Essex chef Jamie Oliver brought this home to
me.

In this series he is wandering around the United States, sampling food as he goes from area to area. In this particular episode he journeyed to Los Angeles and met up with groups of people in the poorer areas of the city. These people, although generally enjoying a very close knit family life also live with murder and gang warfare on a daily basis. There are few families that have not lost a member through violence, and this violence has been rampant for decades.

Areas like this are statistically likely to remain dangerous and poor. While this is, of course, a hugely complicated issue that brings social questions into play along with self-worth, revenge mentality, perceived hurt and class structure, it is also worth remembering that areas like this see a lot of life and death, which might mean that the wyrd of that area is warped and damaged so that simply living within its' bounds changes your outlook. Just as places like Avebury engender a positive 'feel', places like this area of L. A. invoke fear and distrust, not necessarily because of what happens, but as a result of what has happened so intensely for many years.

Wyrd in this instance has become a feedback loop, one that resists change without profound effort. To see how this can happen, we shall have to look at a much bigger picture.

Going Global

With this chapter we are heading back towards the realms of science, much as we did in chapter 2. The difference this time is that we are looking at things on a slightly larger scale than we did previously. We are also heading rather further back in time that we have so far.

Approximately four and a half billion years ago our planet formed from a disc of matter pulled into place by our young sun. Shortly after this the fledgling Earth was hit by a Mars-sized object which shattered it – a violent start for a young planet. This impact was not, in the long term, such a bad thing however as it left in its wake a companion for the Earth – the moon. Considerably closer than it is now the moon's gravity caused massive disruption to the hardening surface of the Earth. After a while things settled down, although the planet was still being bombarded by comets and meteors, making it a lively place but also bringing water in vast quantities. By three point seven billion years ago the Earth had cooled sufficiently for water to remain liquid and for an atmosphere to have formed. And then, three and a half billion years ago something remarkable happened. Chemicals already abundant in the early seas formed themselves into long chains and developed the neat trick of copying themselves. Very, very soon after that the first true life emerged in the form of simple bacteria.

Within half a billion years these simple bacteria had evolved a new trick – they could photosynthesise, pulling the energy they required directly from sunlight rather than having to rely on external chemical reactions. This has several benefits for those organisms able to do this. It means that they need never really go hungry, for one. It also means that they can protect themselves with a very effective form of chemical weapon. One of the by-products of photosynthesis is a gas so toxic it is fatal to many forms of life and causes destruction even to inert materials. That gas, which enabled its early proponents to stave off competition is Oxygen.

Quietly, and for a long time, the bacteria continued to evolve, forming little clumps that learnt to cooperate in the form of blue-green algae and pumping out more Oxygen. Within another few hundred million years some of these bacteria had evolved another remarkable survival strategy. They had developed nuclei, central storage filing cabinets for their genetic material. This enabled them to reproduce more accurately, and to swap material with each-other. Things carried on quite steadily for a while – around 2 billion years, until these (by now quite complex) single-celled organisms started acting together, and the first multi-cellular beings developed. Once that had happened life really began to motor. Having conquered the water it moved inland, and the rest we know all too well – although the time scales involved are not generally appreciated.

As a quick example I am going to ask you to hold your arms straight out at shoulder height so that you look like a large letter 'T'. You may have to put the book down first.

Now that your arms are out, imaging that the distance between your outstretched finger tips represents the time that life has been in existence on this planet. If you could take a nail-file and run it once, just once, across the nail on your right-hand middle finger you would neatly remove the last 5,000 years – that's all of recorded human history. The first bacteria would have appeared, incidentally, near your left wrist.

So far so lovely. We have a planet on which life evolves steadily, becoming more complex as time marches on. However...

Things are not as peaceful as this picture would imply. Life does something that would, at first view, be completely

counter-productive. It goes extinct – regularly. There
have been five mass-extinctions since life first struggled
into existence. The most famous is the one that ended
the dinosaurs' reign, some 65 million years ago, but that
was relatively mild compared with some of the others.
Approximately 250 million years ago something like 95%
of all species on Earth were wiped out by causes unknown.
While this is undoubtedly bad news for the species (and even
worse for the individuals) involved, it is actually a very good
thing for the biosphere. The ecological vacuum left after a
huge extinction event allows new species to evolve, or at least
allows species that survived free reign to really go for it. It was
a direct result of the extinction of the dinosaurs that mammals
(including, eventually, us) came to dominance. Previous
extinctions also allowed similar evolutionary explosions to
happen. It should be pointed out that the current rate of
species-loss is being hailed by some biologists as the sixth
great extinction. The difference, of course, is that we humans
are responsible for the vast majority of this decline this time -
the only time in history when one species has directly caused
the extinction of others; not a proud heritage.

Before we go any further I need to say a little bit about
evolution. This is not the place to embark on a long,
protracted scientific explanation of the processes of speciation
and there are numerous books that do just that far better and
written by authors far better qualified to do the subject justice;
Richard Dawkins' "The Blind Watchmaker" is an excellent
example. However, in order to continue with this particular
train of thought I do need to explain, on a very basic level,
what evolution is.

Charles Darwin, in his seminal book "On the Origin of
Species" set out the case for the Theory of Evolution over a
hundred years ago. He explained very clearly what evolution
was, although he could not explain how it happened. It would
take until 1953 for that part of the theory to be brought to

light, with a discovery in Cambridge that shook the worlds
of chemistry and biology for it was then that James Watson
and Francis Crick announced that they had discovered the
structure of DNA. This discovery enabled biologists to work
out what DNA did and how it did it. It also provided the
missing information that enabled the Theory of Evolution to
work.

Evolution is, essentially, driven by two things. The first is
random genetic mutation. DNA is remarkable stuff. For a
start it is a huge molecule. There is nearly 2 metres of DNA
wrapped up in every single cell (more or less) of your body,
and for many years after its discovery it had no purpose that
anyone could fathom. It just sat there, copying itself diligently
every time a cell divided. By itself it did nothing. With
Watson and Crick's discovery scientists suddenly realised that
DNA wasn't just copied with every cell division – it was the
agent for that division. More than that, it controlled nearly
every action within the cell by producing proteins that act
as instructions for other structures within the cell. By this
process it guides the construction and function of every part
of your body. It is fantastically effective at copying itself, and
has complex mechanisms to ensure that copies are correct.
However, they are not foolproof and, every once in a while,
errors creep in to the copies. Normally they make little or no
difference, but occasionally they can make a change to the
organism they belong to.

Most of the time these changes, genetic mutation, have a
detrimental effect – causing the organism to suffer or to have a
shortened life. However...

Genetic change is only part of the story. The other part
is much bigger. Organisms evolve to best suit the world in
which they live. Those that manifest traits which enable them
to survive and reproduce pass those traits on and the species
continues, happily living in the world in which it has evolved.

If that world changes, however, things can get messy.

One example is very pertinent to you, dear reader. Apes are tree-dwelling creatures. They are happiest when scampering along branches or leaping gracefully from bough to bough. They tend to be miserable when forced to stay on the ground for any length of time because they are not really built for life on terra firma. Their pelvis is the wrong shape, their backs are not really up to the job of supporting their heads when upright, their legs are too short to make real headway and they cannot see over tall grass, meaning that they are prone to the awful number of other organisms that are very well (and toothily) adapted to catch and eat them.

All these problems are not an issue provided the apes are able to stay in the trees. What if the trees disappear? What if climatic change turns forest into savannah? Do the apes suddenly become tiger food?

Largely, yes.

But, all it takes is for an ape to be born with a genetic variation that means that its pelvis is slanted slightly or that its back is more upright. This would not be a good thing in the trees as it would reduce flexibility, but on the ground it gives the creature a far better view of the surrounding area, and therefore a higher chance of surviving the toothy attentions of the other animals in the vicinity, which means that the chances of it surviving to breed are increased. Should that happen there is a good chance that the genes responsible for that minor adaptation are passed onto its offspring. Over time the mutation becomes more pronounced as it is more successful at being passed from generation to generation until the point comes when the resulting animal is vastly different from the animal that originally gave rise to it.

This happens over many generations. This is how evolution produces new species - genetic change and environmental pressure. What is important as far as this discussion is concerned is that it is both random and non-random. Genetic mutation is random. Environmental change is random. The change in genes across a population following these events is not random.

So, organisms evolve to suit the environment. This implies a one-way flow of information, after all only man has developed the ability to alter its world on a large scale, that is, after all, one of the things that makes us unique.

In 1979 James Lovelock published a book that detailed an hypothesis which challenged this idea. He called his idea "Gaia" and it suggested that the Earth itself could be thought of as an organism capable of regulating itself in such a way as to ensure the best possible conditions for life to exist. Seemingly at odds with perceived scientific wisdom he went on to work on a demonstration of the mechanism involved in his hypothesis and, in 1983 he produced a simple computer program called "Daisyworld".

In the first versions of Daisyworld a planet is populated by white and black flowers. The planet also receives a fluctuating amount of heat and light from its sun. Initially the white flowers, which have a slightly higher reproductive rate, proliferate. As they spread across the planet's surface however, they reflect more of the sun's energy back into space, cooling the planet down. Eventually the temperature cools to the point where the white flowers can no longer survive and they begin to die off. This allows the black flowers, who are able to survive lower temperatures than the white, to spread. Over time they out-compete the white flowers and replace them and, as they are black, they absorb more of the sun's heat and the planet warms up. At some point the planet warms to the point that the black flowers can't cope and white flowers start to take over again. This cycle repeats itself several times until an equilibrium is eventually reached. Eventually however, the combined strength of the flowers is not enough to cope with the ever-changing output of the sun and the world suffers a mass extinction.

More complex versions of the program were subsequently developed that added different flowers, rabbits and foxes and eventually built, as computing power developed, into simple but complete ecosystems. All ended up with the same result – eventual stability. In fact, the more complex the simulated ecosystem became the more stable the environment remained. Extinctions still happened, but the periods of stability were longer.

And now (at last, you say) we approach the point as, although obviously not natural, Daisyworld does highlight some important and interesting aspects of wyrd.

Looking back over the previous chapters you should have a pretty good concept of wyrd on a personal level, with its watchwords of responsibility, inter-connectivity and freedom of choice. However, wyrd is much bigger than that. Looking back at the Ball of String Theory we get the idea that wyrd makes, and is made by, networks of interactions – that it is the process of living that makes and defines our wyrd on an individual level, but that even on that level we influence, and are in turn influenced by, those around us.

This is all well and good on a small-scale, personal, local level, but the lessons of Daisyworld and Gaia resonate through the concepts of wyrd.

Wyrd is a product of life; and not just human life. The Anglo-Saxon way of looking at the world, prior to Christianity at any rate, was to see everything as possessing soul – and by definition anything that has soul has its own wyrd. To the Anglo-Saxon observer everything that can be seen was alive in some way or other, and if it is alive then its' wyrd must connect with and alter the wyrd of the observer. Seeing this from a modern perspective enables us to see all life as interconnected. Nothing happens in isolation, and this is being borne out as we gain a deeper understanding of ecology. Wyrd connects us directly to the world around us and our actions, however small, reverberate globally and our actions provide a feedback into the environment in much the same way as the virtual inhabitants of Daisyworld.

This links back to the end of the previous chapter, and the social issues around areas that never seem to be able to change. Looking at these places with the knowledge that wyrd acts as a conduit for expectations and possibilities as well as for events that have already been shaped it is not surprising that those places that endure violence and hardship are smothered by the shapes of the inhabitants wyrd, and that this effect resists change. The lives of those people in that area become shaped by wyrd that has itself been distorted by the lives of those very people. It becomes a dreadful positive-feedback loop where violence and pain feed more violence and pain.

Reading Wyrd

Now that we've spent some time exploring wyrd we come to the part of the book that no doubt many of you leapt straight to. If you did, then please stop, go back and read the first part – it's quite interesting and you might enjoy it, and it is also vital to understanding what the runes are all about.

By now you should have a good idea of what wyrd is. You may also have reached the point of shouting "So???".

Wyrd is not passive. Neither is it active. It has no personality, wishes or desires. It is however, all encompassing and weaves its way into all aspects of life. It helps form our thoughts and adds colour to our decisions and as such it is altered by our trials and successes, can influence our outlook and can alter our perception of events. Finding a way to read its patterns can provide deep insight into the subconscious and can help resolve issues that may be deeply buried but that which still effect a control on our lives.

There is a way of reading wyrd that developed alongside the understanding of it as a concept, that is interlinked with it. That method is the runes.

What are Runes?

Runes are an alphabetic script used by the peoples of Northern Europe from the first century CE until well into the Middle Ages.

In addition to their use as a written alphabet, the runes also served as a system of symbols used for magic and divination. Runes fell into disuse as the Roman alphabets became the preferred script of most of Europe, but their forms and meanings were preserved in inscriptions and manuscripts.

The primary characteristic which distinguishes a runic alphabet from other alphabets is that each letter, or rune, has a meaning. Runes also have magical and religious significance as well, thus transforming the simple process of writing into a magical act. They are also used for divinatory readings and to create magical spells.

Today, runes have been rediscovered as a symbolic system and have gained immense popularity as a means of divination. However, they are much more than a curious alternative to Tarot cards for telling fortunes. They provide a key to understanding the lives and beliefs of the ancient people who created them, and have much to teach us about a way of life that was perhaps more intimately connected to the natural world, and to the realm of spirit, than our own.

History and Origin of the Runes

What we now know as the runic alphabet seems to have developed from two distinct sources - one magical, one literate. Pre-runic symbols, or hällristningar, have been found in various Bronze Age rock carvings, primarily in Sweden. Some of these symbols are readily identifiable in the later alphabets, while others represent ideas and concepts which were incorporated into the names of runes (sun, horse, etc.). The exact meanings of these sigils are now lost to us, as is their original purpose, but they are believed to have been used for divination or lot-casting, and it is fairly certain that they contributed to the magical function of the later runic alphabets.

There is some debate over the origin of the "alphabet" aspect of the runes. Cases have been made for both Latin and Greek derivation, but historical and archaeological evidence strongly indicates a Northern Italic origin. The parallels between the two alphabets are too close to be ignored, particularly in the forms of the letters, as well as in the variable direction of the writing. This would also explain why so many of the runes resemble Roman letters, since both Italic and Latin scripts are derived from the Etruscan alphabet (itself a branch of the Western Greek family of alphabets).

This theory would place the original creation of the futhark sometime before the 1st. Century CE, when the Italic scripts were absorbed and replaced by the Latin alphabet. Linguistic and phonetic analysis points to an even earlier inception date, perhaps as far back as 200 BCE

When the northern tribes began integrating the Italic alphabet into their own symbolic system, they gave the letters names relating to all aspects of their secular and religious lives, thus transforming their simple pictographs into a magical alphabet which could be used for talismans, magical inscriptions and divination.

The name "futhark", like the word "alphabet", is derived from the first few letters in the runic sequence, which differs considerably of the Latin alphabet and is unique amongst alphabetic scripts. The futhark originally consisted of 24 letters, beginning with F and ending with D, and was used by the northern Germanic tribes of Sweden, Norway, Denmark, and Northern Germany. This form of the runes is known as the Elder, or Germanic Futhark.

Sometime around the fifth century AD, changes occurred in the runes in Frisia (the area around the northern Netherlands and north-western Germany). This period coincided with the Anglo-Saxon invasions from this area and the appearance of similar runes in the British Isles. The forms of several of the runes changed, notably the runes for A/O, C/K, H, J, S, and Ng. Also, changes in the language led to between five and nine runes being added to the alphabet to compensate for the extra sounds, and several runes were given different corresponding letters. This alphabet has become known as the Anglo-Saxon Futhorc.

In Scandinavia, the Elder Futhark remained in use until some time around the eighth century (the time of the Eddas), when changes the Old Norse language occurred, and corresponding changes in the runic alphabet were made to accommodate the new sounds. However, unlike the Anglo-Saxon Futhorc, the Younger Futhark (as it is now called) reduced the number of from 24 to 16, and several runes came to represent multiple sounds. The forms of the runes were also changed and simplified. There are several variations of this futhark - Danish, long branch, Norwegian, dotted, etc.

It is possible that they were also brought to North America with the Vinland expeditions, but so far no authenticated inscriptions have been found.

The Runic Revival

The runes, primarily in their Younger form, remained in common use until well into the 17th Century. Up until this time, they were everything from coins to coffins, and in some places their use was actually sanctioned by the Church.

Even the common knew simple runic spells, and the runes were frequently consulted on matters of both public and private interest. Unfortunately, with the magical arts, they were officially banned in 1639 as part of the Church's efforts to "drive the devil out of with Europe". The rune masters were either executed or went underground, and the knowledge of the runes may well have died with them. Some that the knowledge was passed on in secret, but it is almost impossible to separate ancient traditions from more modern esoteric philosophies in such cases.

Perhaps the darkest period in the history of runic studies was their revival by German scholars connected with the Nazi movement in the that 20's and 30's. What began as a legitimate folkloric resurgence unfortunately became so tainted by Nazi ideology and racism that the research from this period was rendered all but useless to any serious student of runic lore.

After the Second World War, the runes fell into dis-favour as a result of their association with Naziism, and very little was written about them until the fifties and sixties. It was not until the mid-eighties, with the widespread appeal of the "New Age" movement and revival of Pagan religions (especially the Asatru movement) that the runes regained their popularity as both a divinatory system and a tool for self-awareness.

The Meanings of the Runes

There are several historical runic inscriptions, found on everything from swords to stones to bronze pendants, which list the entire runic alphabet in order. One of the oldest and most complete of these is the Kylver stone, found in Gotland, Sweden and dating from the fifth century CE Others are less complete, but show a remarkable continuity in the order in which the runes until are listed. The only surviving written accounts of the actual names and meanings of the runes, however, were not recorded until the advent of the Christian era. Some of these manuscripts, which date from the 9th. Century until well into 12th, are known as rune poems. These poems have a verse for each rune, each of which begins with the rune itself and its name. Some of these poems are more Pagan than others, particularly those from Iceland, where Christianity was not yet as widespread as it was in the Anglo-Saxon regions.

The rune names themselves appear to have been passed down relatively intact, and although no manuscript exists listing the names of the older, Germanic runes, the Anglo-Saxon and Scandinavian rune poems agree to such an extent that their common origin can be deduced. These names are probably our best clue as to what the individual runes actually meant to the people that used them.

Interpretation

I tend to approach the futhark as a journey - a spiritual odyssey in which the traveller encounters obstacles, receives gifts, learns vital lessons that will aid in their development as a human being. This process is at once personal and mythic, following cycles and patterns that reflect the Norse and Anglo-Saxon world-view. This world-view was fundamentally different from that of the average 20th century Westerner, so a thorough understanding of the myths, culture and lifestyle of the ancient peoples of northern Europe is a complete understanding of the runes. Please see the online resources on these subjects, as well as my recommended reading list for more information.

It should be noted that the following interpretations of the meanings of the runes, while firmly founded in historical evidence and understanding of the Anglo-Saxon culture, are at least partially speculative and should not be taken as the "True and Original Meanings of the Runes". Given that so little is actually known about the runes, it is to be expected that even the most cynical scholar writing about them will inevitably bring their own theories and biases to their subject. I am no exception. To make things a little clearer, I have tried to distinguish hard fact from my own speculation wherever possible.

I use the Elder futhark for divination. However, I tend to use the Anglo-Saxon poems for interpretation because they are more akin to the English way of thinking. There are no real differences in meaning between the various poems although the names of the runes do change.

I have included the Anglo-Saxon poems for each rune.

The Blank Rune

Many books use a 'blank' rune to symbolise wyrd. A moments thought will reveal that this cannot be traditional (in fact it was made up in 1982 by Ralph Blum). The runes are a writing system, not Scrabble. How can you have a non-letter in an alphabet?

If you own a set with a blank rune, please remove it before casting the runes – you don't need it and it will serve only to confuse you.

Runes and Tarot

There have been several attempts to link the runes and Tarot. They are, after all, both divinatory systems and they have a similar number of archetypes - 28 for the Major Arcana of the Tarot, 24-31 for the runes depending on the futhark being used. That is, however, the only similarity between them.

Historically, tarot is a newcomer. The use of the cards for esoteric purposes dates from 1781 – prior to this date they were (and still are) simply playing cards. A Swiss clergyman and freemason, Antoine Court de Gebelin assigned archetypal meanings to the picture cards of the deck, called them 'tarot' and invented an identification with the ancient Egyptians.

There is a bigger problem in associating the Tarot with the runes, however. When reading the cards you are never able to provide your own interpretation unless you have developed your own artwork. You will always be working with an artists interpretation of the meanings of the cards. The runes are simple scratched shapes and contain, in most cases, no clues as to their meaning. You are reliant on a completely different method of interpretation - namely the rune poems and the subtleties contained therein. You have no other reliable source (even this book is subject to my interpretation of the poems based on my own experience).

Having said that, the runes and tarot both 'work'. They are both able to provide psychological insight. Linking the two however is a false idea that weakens both. They work on different levels of interpretation and the meanings of the Major Arcana and the runes are different. The runes have no 'reversed' position and should only rarely be read individually. Indeed, any attempt to merge the two is the result of poor research and understanding of both systems.

The Runic Journey

While the meanings of the runes are useful psychological tools when taken individually they really come into their own when viewed as a metaphor for spiritual and mental growth.

The 24 runes of the Elder Futhark can be broken into three sections, known as Aetts. Each Aett helps plot a course through the many challenges that life can throw at us. Looking at the runes as a journey in this way can also help with interpretation. Some of the stanzas of the rune poems are rather obscure to modern eyes, and seeing the flow of the runes helps put them into context.

The First Aett

We start at the point where Western Society seems to stop. Feoh is the rune of money and wealth. However, it is not a rune of accumulation; in fact it contains very explicit instructions on what to do with your money. Should you find yourself with an abundance, it says, share it, for that is the only way to gain honour. So, while initially seen as a rune of money, Feoh is actually a rune of wealth, not money– a rune of acceptance of comfort and the need to stop striving for extravagance. In order to move on in the journey – in fact in order to move to just the next stage, the lesson to learn is that the mundane world is not enough on its own. However, there is no clue within this rune as to how to move on. In order to do that you have to leap forward with no further information.

The leap is not physical, it is psycho-spiritual. The next rune is both the leap and the result. The ability to see life purely on emotion and passion opens up new realms of understanding, and Ur delivers that in spades. Ur is the rune of the fight, of the rite of passage. It is the strength needed to leap from the mundane to the spiritual, to overcome obstacles and prejudice. It is also the rune of recklessness, and leaping too often without looking will, at some point, land you in trouble.

Thorn, the next stage of our journey, the result of that once-too-often leap of faith. It is the briar-patch – those times in life when everything is pain and there is no easy way out. Every move brings new trials as a result of our own actions. While leaping blindly was the only way to move on from Feoh, that option has gone – movement of any kind hurts. Now is a time for reflection.

Os provides that in a very no-nonsense way. Os is Odin's rune, and he is the god who dreamed the runes into being. Os is the ability to examine the self honestly, questioning oneself deeply and acknowledging the answers that come back. It is the first stage of true self-knowledge. This kind of introspection will inevitably lead to changes of thought, and that is the next stage.

Rad asks us a simple question. Is our perception of events accurate? It may be that they are, but one should always check, for that enables and develops empathy. A simple message with deep and profound implications. With that level of understanding we can move on.

But not far. We have gained an understanding of ourselves, and many people never progress beyond Rad in their journey (many never even get that far), and the next rune, Ken, reminds us of how little we still know. Ken is a rune of knowledge, but only partial. It is the state of being in a darkened hall with a torch, only able to make out detail but never able to see the whole picture. However, those details, coupled with the empathy of Rad open our minds and hearts to complete the lesson begun with Feoh. Gyfu is the runeof giving without expectation. It enables us to realise that helping those who are less fortunate than us gives us dignity, and wit that dignity and self-worth comes joy. Wynn, the final rune in the first Aett is an acknowledgement that we have reached a stage where we can relax and breathe, taking stock of the journey so far and enjoying the view – albeit temporarily.

We have learned a lot from the first Aett, but it has all been centred around the self. The second Aett throws things at us that we need to cope with, things that are external to us and that can prove overwhelming if we haven't attained the understanding from the first Aett.

From the peace and quiet of Wynn, all hell breaks loose as we are hit by the storm of Haegl. Where Thorn hurt us by inability, Haegl is indicative of those times when life throws us from pillar to post, never letting us stop or rest, constantly demanding our strength. These are events from outside our sphere of influence, the times when wyrd is against us and shows itself by destruction. However, such activity cannot last forever, and eventually it gives way to somethingmore insidious. Such times often leave us feeling troubled and incomplete, Nyd is the rune of this period – a time when we are constantly needled by nagging doubts. While understanding those doubts or needs will enable us to move on, that movement will be slow, as the storm encountered at Haegl solidifies into ice, and we are unable to move freely. The period of enforced stagnation can be harsh to those used to action, but Is brings its own warning. Any attempt to force the situation will result in events careering off out of control again. It is best to learn to stop and wait, for nothing remains at a standstill for ever, and ice has a beauty of its own if one takes the time to appreciate it.

From the enforced imprisonment of Is, Ger enables us to move at last. However, it is a reminder that we achieve through hard work and patience. Nothing worthwhile happens immediately. If we are not careful though we will remain at this stage – caught in the cycle of the year, which, although not necessarily bad, would be a shame. The next stage however, requires real motivation on our part, and is not easy.

We first encountered Odin in the first Aett. Here he takes

centre stage, as Eoh is the process he underwent to gain the knowledge of the runes. According to the mythology he hung for nine days and nights before undergoing a shamanic vision in which he took up the runes. Eoh is that process of gaining deep understanding of the self. This sort of knowledge is never gained without sacrifice, and is not guaranteed. It requires a willingness to examine oneself honestly and deeply and to be prepared to uncover parts of the psyche that have been locked away for years. This process happens probably only a few times during a life.

One of the lessons that can come from Eoh is the understanding that there are times when waiting is the best course of action. Unlike the forced wait of Is though, the period of stasis Peorth brings is watchful and intended. With Peorth we understand that there are times when leaping into the fray is the worst thing to do, at least until the time is right. It may be hard, but biding one's time is a useful skill to learn.

While we are sat watching it is a good idea to ensure that we are protected from those who may wish to take advantage of our inactivity. Eohl grants that protection. While there is no direct warning with Eohl, just as there was none with Ur, this protection should be used sparingly. While Ur can lead to recklessness, Eohl can lead to being too closed off. Allowing nobody through defences leads to isolation and, should that happen, your journey stops here. Attempting to control every situation will only cause pain, and learning to go with the flow is important. Sigel teaches us that there are times when simply allowing the currents of life to carry us is the best action. If our defences are too strong we will never be able to move with Sigel, and we will never be borne to land.

The second Aett has taught us that life is unpredictable, painful and that sometimes allowing it to happen to and around us is the best course of action. He third Aett shows us how to fight back.

We left the second Aett allowing the course of eventsto guide us, going with the flow. Tiw, the first rune of the third Aett enables us to change direction as we wish, withan important caveat. Tiw is the strength of the warrior, the ability to overcome any situation. However, Tiw also sacrificed his hand in his final battle, so this strength comes at a price. Sacrifices need to be made in order to control situations, and these sacrifices are real. Just giving something up that will not really be missed is not a sacrifice.

If you can do this, then real creativity and openness of thinking is the result. Beorc enables us to grow and start new ventures, safe in the knowledge that we are willing to cast off old perceptions or habits in order to achieve what we are capable of.

In order for this creativity to really take flight we can learn from the past, in particular we can re-visit the energy of Ur. But we have grown and can now harness that raw power and bend it to a useful purpose. This is what Eh allows us. Passion and strength harnessed and bridled.

All this can make us feel pretty indestructible, and the next rune brings us down to Earth. Man is a warning, pure and simple. If you think too much of yourself, or rely too heavily on others, prepare to be let down. Everyone has their own wyrd and they will, at some stage, have to do their own thing, regardless of the effects on you.

The realisation that we are, ultimately, only able to rely on ourselves produces fear. That fear is expressed in the next rune, Lagu. However, although this fear is very real it is temporary. We have learned that we are capable of anything we put our minds to, although it will not be ease. We have learned that we are capable of new beginnings. What we need to do now is prepare the ground, plough the soil for our new self to grow. This is the role of Ing.

This preparation bears fruit in Othel. Othel is Feoh made real. It is the security of hearth and home, a place of happiness and comfort. We have learnt all the lessons we need and can now relax.

Finally we can greet a new dawn of self, a day of completion, light and warmth made real by Daeg. However, this may only lead to complacency and the journey starts again.

It is important to realise that the order of the futhark only describes a potential progression. In fact, most people will stop at one point for many years or will possible be at two or three simultaneously. As ever, the important thing to note is the patterns that life makes, not necessarily the position one happens to be at within that pattern.

Recognising the position you are at within that progression is important, however. Whether it is the painof Thorn or the joy of Wynn you should be constantly reminding yourself that the pattern of your wyrd is constantly in flux and that while you may be stuck at this moment, that shape will change. This is where self analysis becomes useful, and also where the runes can come into their own as a tool that can enable you in reading the shifting patterns of your wyrd.

Working with the runes

Fairly obviously, the first part of working with the runes is to learn them. While you do not necessarily need to learn them by heart in order to read them, it will improve the flow and feel of a reading if you do not have to refer back to a book.

The important part of each rune description is the poem. The poems contain a degree of subtlety that is difficult to put into words any other way, and the verses of the poem should be referred to in preference over the text.

The next stage is to attempt a cast. Many books advocate using tarot spreads for the runes, however the traditional method of reading them was to drop or throw the full set onto a cloth. When you consider that the runes are meant to show the patterns of wyrd you will also realise that reading runes singly means that you miss out on the complexity that life throws up. You read patterns, not individual runes.

Another anomaly advocated by many books is that the runes have different meanings depending on whether they are upright or not. Several things make this idea nonsensical.

The runes were developed as an alphabet. Placing letters upside down makes no sense. There is no mention of this idea anywhere in the rune poems. If you are casting the runes rather than placing them, they will land randomly. Sorting out which should be upright and which reversed therefore becomes impossible. The meanings of the runes are generally not black and white. They contain caveats and warnings, lessons and trials. Simply saying that Thorn reversed mean happy times is to ignore the poem and the subtlety of interpretation that the runes require.

Casting can be difficult as it can present a massive amount of information in one hit. However, it is a very good starting point for an in-depth reading as it will give an overview of the questioner's life in.

The cast itself is very straightforward - simply tip all the runes from the pouch into the client's hands. It is important at this stage that they do not focus on a particular question, that they just allow their consciousness to withdraw within themselves so that you get a reading about their whole life. Then they scatter the runes, dropping them from a height of around six inches above the cloth.

Discard any which fall upside down. Any which landon their edges or outside the cloth may be discarded. The difficulty is that there will generally be quite a few runes left on the cloth. Try not to get too bogged-down with extracting every possible meaning from every possible combination. As you are reading you should find that some relationships are more important than others. You should find that patterns emerge and become apparent as you are talking throughthe reading - these patterns will most likely change as you describe what you are seeing, throwing more light onto specific areas of the querant's life.

I tend to view those towards the centre as being actual issues or problems while those around the edges tend to show the solutions (in general terms) or the possible ways to counteract whatever is bugging you.

Once you have a good general idea of the situation (and clients will add more or less to the reading as they see fit) you should be able to pick out those areas which require further digging to resolve. At this point pack all the runes back into the pouch and ask your client to think of the situation thatis most pressing, and then to pick out three runes in quick succession.

These runes show the situation in more detail, andwill often provide some indication of the course of action required to change the pattern of wyrd in order to resolveit. This step may be repeated a couple of times to gain more clarity around particular situations. I tend to finish by asking the client to pick out one rune as a talisman - something to remember and focus on for the future.

Interpreting the patterns is a skill that comes with time, but it does not require ritual to accomplish.

Working with People

When you read for someone else you may end up uncovering aspects of their life that they have taken many years to bury. As a reader you are, albeit temporarily, acting as a counsellor and integrity and professionalism are paramount. There is a good chance that clients will open up to you in a way that they will not do for family or friends, simply because you are in a position of authority and the fact that there is a good chance they will never see you again. This is an important point to remember. You have a duty of care, however fleeting, to your client. That duty of care means that you should be honest. You will not help by agreeing with their version of events if the runes (and your own intuition) are telling you something different.

Similarly, you need to assess whether your client who, it must be remembered, has come to you for help and guidance, is ready to receive and deal with the issues you may bring up. Anyone who comes to you will generally fall into one of two categories:-

1. General interest. This person has possibly had Tarot readings before but knows very little about the runes and comes to you because the runes are a bit different.

2. In need of help. This person will either contact you directly out of the blue or will find you some other way.

Psychic fayres are a good place to get your name out and this is the sort of person who you will generally encounterat these events. This person does not know anything about the runes and may come to you last, after looking round everyone else. This person is the reason you are there. They may well have deep-rooted problems that recur constantlyin their lives. They may well have gone to psychics and mediums before, but they have come to you now because there is something about the runes that is grounded and earthy – something that means that they will get the truth, warts and all. They need help in assessing a situation or guidance in getting out of one. A fear of orthodox medicine or a lack of real acknowledgement of a problem has led them to come today.

Either way, an empathic understanding of people is useful. Sympathy for situations is pointless, you are not your client and feeling sorry for them will not help. Empathy on the other hand, enables you to put yourself in their shoes for the duration of a reading, to interpret the runes in light of their wyrd (and not your own as a sympathetic reading would produce). Don't be afraid of their pain and sorrow – always have a box of tissues handy. You can help resolve issues, or at least encourage a new way of thinking about them.

On a final note, always remember that your client's problems are real, regardless of whether you would find them easy to deal with or not. It is their wyrd – the sum of their life – that has brought them to you. If it were a happy life they would most likely not be sat in front of you in the first place.

Successional readings can leave one feeling drained and taking some time out after a couple of readings, particularly if you are driving anywhere, is a good policy. Needless to say, drinking and divination are not good bedfellows

Wealth is a comfort to all men;

yet must every man bestow it freely,

if he wish to gain honour in the sight of the Lord.

Fehu

Fehu is the first letter of the futhark and the starting point of the runic journey. Of itself it is a very straightforward rune to interpret - standing simply for money. However, there isa warning here. As this is the first rune it reminds us that wyrd is forever responsive to our actions and intentions. This reminder is not repeated with every rune, but the Anglo-Saxon Rune Poem is very clear with this one.

While it is important to have enough wealth to live comfortably such wealth brings with it an obligation to see that those not so fortunate as ourselves are cared for. In doing so a person gains in stature and helps to straighten out the kinks in wyrd that may arise from selfishness.

FEHU : wealth

Phonetic equivalent: f

The aurochs is proud and has great horns;
it is a very savage beast and fights with its horns;
a great ranger of the moors, it is a creature of mettle.

Ur

The aurochs was a species of wild ox, similar to a bison, that was once found all over Europe, but which became extinct sometime in the 17th. Century. They were said to be slightly smaller than elephants, and had horns as long as six feet, which were highly prized by the Germanii as drinking horns. Paintings of aurochs have been found in Neolithic caves, and it believed that the aurochs hunt had some significance as a rite of passage for a boy entering manhood. The aurochs is the epitome of the wild animal, as opposed to the domesticated cattle represented by fehu.

Ur is the rune of the God of the sacred hunt and his shaman/priest. Following the kind of mundane, day today survival represented by fehu, it is the first recognition by mankind of the divine in nature, and his first attempt to control it through the use of sympathetic magic. It also represents an awareness of death and our own mortality, which may well be the only thing which truly distinguishes us from other animals. The energy of this rune is raw, powerful, and distinctly masculine, in the sense that it is first pure, elemental fire. The boy who has killed the aurochs has just entered manhood, and has therefore been initiated into the first level of the mysteries - the awareness that the source of life is death.

The caution of this rune is to be aware of recklessness.

UR : aurochs

Phonetic equivalent: u

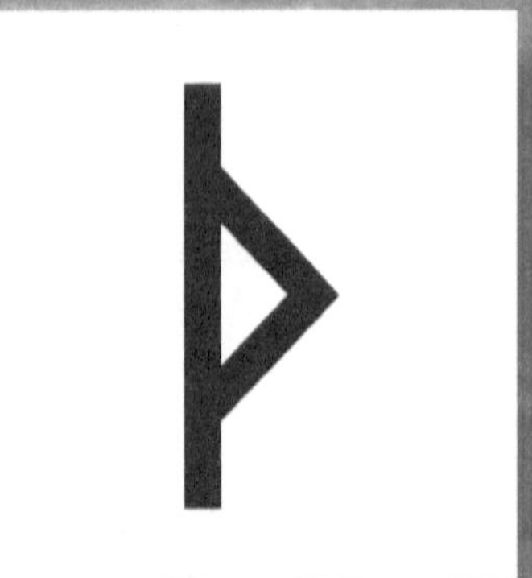

The thorn is exceedingly sharp,
an evil thing for any knight to touch,
uncommonly severe on all who sit among them.

Thorn

The lesson of this rune is 'to learn you must suffer', meaning not only literal suffering, but also in the biblical sense of 'allowing' - allowing one's destiny to unfold asit should, and allowing one's self to experience all thatlife offers us. What may at first appear to be a negative, destructive event, may well turn out to contain an important lesson. The Giants may seem to be evil and destructive to the Aesir, but they bring about change, and eventually clear the way for a new age.

In the journey represented by the futhark many people get stuck on this stage of their lives, repeating the events surrounding pain or hardship again and again - not learning the lessons that have led to this position.

THORN : thorn

Phonetic equivalent: th (as in "thing")

*The mouth is the source of all language,
a pillar of wisdom and a comfort to wise men,
a blessing and a joy to every knight.*

Os

This rune represents the instinctive, primal energy of ur tempered with the discipline and experience of thorn. These elements are combined in the personage of Odin, who exhibits the characteristics of both chieftain and shaman-a god of wisdom as well as war. Odin is also a shaman, travelling between the worlds on his eight-legged horse, Sleipnir.

Os is a rune of communication and understanding. This is the rune of teachers. Most people stay at this point in their lives, having learned to deal with pain and what life can throw at them and having gained a degree of self-knowledge required to prevent similar events occurring again.

On the runic journey this rune represents the initial stages of communicating with the self - the first part of gaining self understanding.

OS : mouth

Phonetic equivalent: a (as in "fall")

*Riding seems easy to every warrior while he is indoors
and very courageous to him who traverses the high-roads
on the back of a stout horse.*

Rad

Rad shows how changing circumstances alter one's perception of events. On a personal note it can be indicative of complacency whilst examination of someone else's life would interpret the same situation as brave or foolhardy.

A prime example could be someone who stays in a failing relationship. They may be able to see all to clearly what other people in similar situations need to do, but cannot apply that same degree of knowledge to themselves.

It serves as a gentle warning not to be too quick to judge.

RAD : perceptions

Phonetic equivalent: r

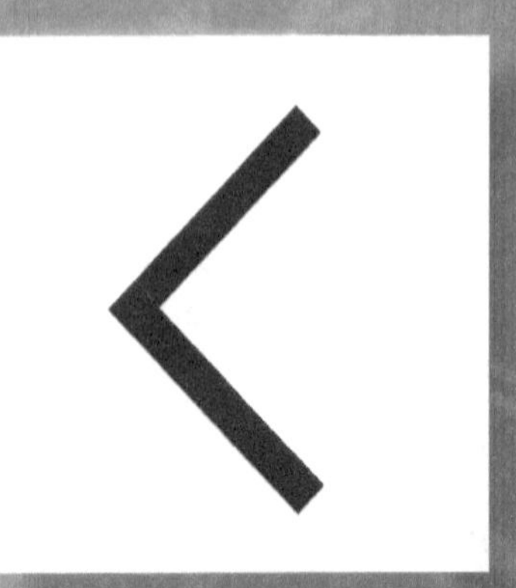

The torch is known to every living man
by its pale, bright flame;
it always burns where princes sit within.

Ken

In modern usage, the Scottish 'ken' means to know or understand, and this is the sense in which the rune should interpreted. Today, light, inspiration and knowledge are often associated, as in 'gaining enlightenment' and 'shedding light on the problem', even in the image of a light bulb going on over someone's head when they get an idea. To bring light is to make the invisible visible.

Unlike the wisdom gained at thorn, ken only allows usto take bits and pieces of this knowledge away with us as we need it. This knowledge will generally come in the form of a sudden inspiration, and we will be able to see clearly the answer that was once hidden from us.

A useful analogy for this rune is to imagine oneself in a dark hall with a torch. The light, although bright, only allows small aspects of the whole to be seen. Focussing on detail can be useful, but it should never be confused with the full picture.

KEN : torch

Phonetic equivalent: c

Generosity brings credit and honour, which support one's dignity;
it furnishes help and subsistence
to all broken men who are devoid of aught else.

Gyfu

Gyfu is a rune of connection, particularly the connections between people. Up until now, our journey has been a solitary one. This rune represents those places where our path intersects with others, and allows us to begin to form conscious relationships. Such relationships are strengthened and sanctified by the exchange of gifts.

The use of the gift as a symbol of an oath or a bond isan ancient one. When a lord wanted to ensure the loyalty of one of his subjects, he would give that person a gift. The gift would create a debt on the part of the person receivingit, and this debt would ensure his readiness to serve his lord. Similarly, a gift given between lovers, especially that of the ring, symbolizes the bond between them. Originally, only the man gave the ring in a marriage for much the same reason as the lord giving gifts to his vassals, but today the arrangement is usually more equitable. Gifts or offerings given to the Gods often carry the same meaning, representing the giver's love for or loyalty to their Gods. The giving of a gift implies the acceptance of a debt with the understanding that the debt will not be repaid. It is this imbalance which forms the bond.

GYFU: gift

Phonetic equivalent: g (as in "girl")

*Bliss he enjoys who knows not suffering, sorrow nor anxiety,
and has prosperity and happiness and a good enough house.*

Wynn

Wynn is the last rune of the first aett, and thus represents both the end of one cycle and preparation for the next. It is a very positive, stable rune, and is another place where people tend to get stalled along their journey. Christian poets related it to heaven, but in fact it more closely resembles the Pagan Valhalla, since this particular paradise is not a permanent one.

Like the wealth of fehu, the glory of wynn is tempered. It is not everlasting bliss, it is the happiness that comes from contentment.

WYNN: joy

Phonetic equivalent: w

H

Hail is the whitest of grain;
it is whirled from the vault of heaven
and is tossed about by gusts of wind
and then it melts into water.

Haegl

Like the Tower in the Tarot, haegl is only a negative rune if we choose to view it in that way, and refuse to learn its lessons. Appearing as it does at the beginning of the second aett, it marks both a beginning and an end, and knocks us out of the safety and complacency of wynn. It represents what a friend of mine used to refer to as the 'flying ladle Fates, syndrome'- that whenever things appear to be going too well, you can expect a good, healthy whack in the head from the Fates, just to make sure you're paying attention.

Unlike the pain of thorn, haegl is drawn from external events rather than internal decisions.

These sorts of 'wake-up calls' from the Gods will happen frequently throughout a person's life, but are often misinterpreted as divine punishment for some imagined wrong when in fact they are merely a way of drawing your attention to a recurrent pattern in your life. Unfortunately, these types of events have a tendency to repeat themselves with greater and greater severity until the lesson is learned and the pattern is broken. For example, someone who needs to break their dependency on a certain type of person will find themselves in relationships with such people over and over again with more and more disastrous results until they recognize the pattern as emanating from themselves and break it willingly.

HAEGL: hail

Phonetic equivalent: h

Nyd

If haegl is a flying ladle, then nyd is the empty pot. It is a gentle, nudging reminder that all is not as it should be. Life appears to be out of synch, and nothing seems to be going right. No matter how much you have, it is never enough, and there is an ever present desire for something more, something better. On the positive side, this dissatisfaction with the status quo can serve to draw one away from the relative safety of wunjo and motivate towards change.

Nyd represents an imbalance between one's desires and one's assets. How you resolve this situation will influence the rest of the journey, but the awareness of the imbalance itself can also be illuminating. It causes you to closely examine and perhaps reassess your values and priorities, and forces you back onto the path of your own happiness.

NYD: need

Phonetic equivalent: n

Ice is very cold and immeasurably slippery;
it glistens as clear as glass and most like to gems;
it is a floor wrought by the frost, fair to look upon.

Is

In modern symbology, fire is generally masculine and ice (or earth) is feminine, but it is unknown whether the Norse shared this association. Certainly, ice was a constant factor in their day to day lives. It threatened their crops and their ships almost throughout the year, but it also served as a symbol of creation, from which all life will eventually spring. It says something about the Norse mind that they could recognize the need to have such a seemingly destructive joining of elements in order to create maintain life. Fire may be warm and pleasant, but it must be balanced by the freezing of winter just as birth must be balanced by death. Even the little death of sleep has been proven to be vital for our mental and physical well-being.

Is encompasses all of these ideas, but primarily represents a period of rest (which may well be enforced by circumstance) before activity, and itself forms the material from which life can be created. The danger is that this rest becomes too easy and will lead to complacency.

IS: ice

Phonetic equivalent: i (as in inch)

Summer is a joy to men, when God, the holy King of Heaven,
suffers the earth to bring forth shining fruits
for rich and poor alike

Ger

In this modern age of central heating and oranges in February, it is difficult to imagine the close ties that people once had with the cycles of the year, particularly in the more Northern climes. The changing seasons affected not only the weather, but also the to day activities and even the diets of ancient peoples. Constant change was the norm, and the object was to become attuned those changes, not to fight against them. An ancient farmer (or even some modern ones) wouldn't need to look at a calendar to tell him when to plant, or read a weather forecast to know when the snows were coming. The changing seasons were a part of his blood and bones, and his very existence depended on adapting to change.

Ger follows is just as spring follows winter. The frozen stagnancy of ice is broken by the turning of the wheel, and things are once again moving along as they should. In fact, we have now broken out of the entire set 'negative' runes with which we began this aett. This has been accomplished not by fighting to escape the ice or railing against the unfairness of fate, but by learning from those experiences and simply waiting for the inevitable thaw. Ger is the communion wine - the product of the joining of opposites bringing life. Storms may come and go, but the sun is always there and life is generally pretty good. Enjoy it while you can.

GER: year, harvest

Phonetic equivalent: y (or j)

The yew is a tree with rough bark,
hard and fast in the earth, supported by its roots,
a guardian of flame and a joy upon an estate

Eoh

The yew tree has been associated with runes, magic
and death in northern and western Europe since time
immemorial. The reasons for this ancient association are
numerous, but seem to principally derive from the fact that
yews are evergreens which retain their greenery even through
the death of winter, and because their red berries are symbolic
of the blood of life. The yew is extremely long-lived, thus
effectively 'immortal'. Reverence for the yew dates back to
before the times of the Celts, and continues today in Christian
tradition.

Eoh is the thirteenth rune in the futhark, and marks the
middle of the alphabet. (It is interesting to note that the Death
card in the Tarot is also the thirteenth card.) This rune is
the turning point in the runic journey, and represents the
transformation the initiatory process. All rites of passage,
particularly those marking the transition into adulthood,
contain the symbolism of death, the idea being that one's
former 'self' has died and given birth to a new persona.

Eoh is the passage through which we must enter the realm
of Hel in order to gain the knowledge and acceptance of
our mortality, as well as those mysteries which can only be
learned from the dark Lady of the dead. The process is a truly
frightening one, but it is something we all must go through if
we are to confront our deepest fears and emerge with the kind
of wisdom that be taught but must be experienced. Eoh is the
gateway to this wisdom, and lies between life (Ger) and rebirth
(peorth).

EOH: yew

Phonetic equivalent: ei

*Peorth is a source of recreation and amusement to the great,
where warriors sit blithely together in the banqueting-hall.*

Peorth

The actual interpretation of peorth has been the subject of much controversy among runic scholars. The problem lies in the fact that the initial P sound doesn't occur anywhere else in the old Germanic language, leading to the belief that the word was imported from another language. The Old English rune poem seems to indicate that it had to do with some sort of game, leading many to interpret it as 'chess pawn' or 'dice-cup'. The dice-cup meaning is particularly interesting as it not only fits the shape of rune, but also hints at such an object's original use as a container for the runes themselves.

The imagery with this rune is of the querant watching a game of dice being enjoyed by a couple of warriors. The watcher wants to join but is also content to observe.

This is the ability to bide one's time, to await the right moment to join the game.

PEORTH: dice-cup

Phonetic equivalent: p

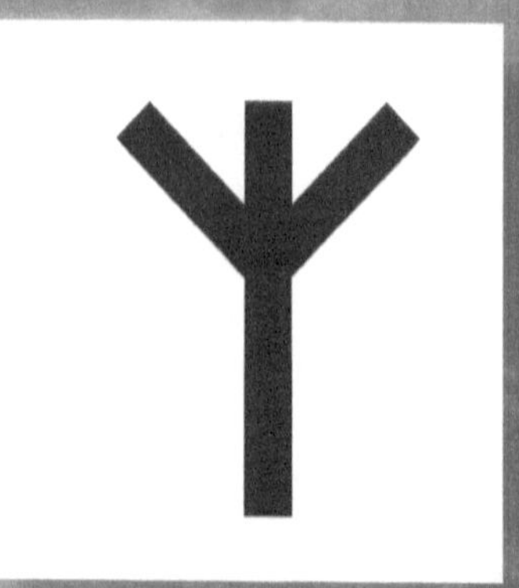

The Eolh-sedge is mostly to be found in a marsh;
it grows in the water and makes a ghastly wound,
covering with blood every warrior who touches it.

Eohl

This is the archetypal rune of protection. It represents sedge-grass, a plant which can cut and wound the unwary.

This form of protection is frequently set up as a result of pain brought about by being too open to events and it can allow respite, a time to lick one's wounds. If it is prominent in a reading it could be indicative of walls being erected too strongly, which can lead to isolation.

Magically, this rune is often used over doors and windows in an attempt to block negative feelings and emotions gaining access.

EOHL: protection

Phonetic equivalent: x, z

The sun is ever a joy in the hopes of seafarers
when they journey away over the fishes' bath,
until the courser of the deep bears them to land.

Sigel

The sun is held sacred by almost every religion in the world. Its light and warmth symbolize life and growth and all that is good. Norse cosmology describes the sun being driven around the heavens in a chariot and chased by a great wolf, which will devour at Ragnarok. Throughout Indo-European Paganism, the sun has frequently been associated with the horse, often described as being carted around the sky by a horse. Both are symbolic of life and fertility, and are usually considered 'masculine' in polarity, although in Norse myth the chariot is driven by a girl. The swastika or sun wheel is a constant motif in rock carvings dating Neolithic times, and occurs throughout Europe and Asia. The sun rune itself is a variation on this symbol, and represents motion and energy.

Sigel marks the end of the second aett, and like wynn represents success and glory. However, unlike the rest and relaxation of Valhalla, the sun is very much an active symbol. We have reached the end of the aett successfully, and the conclusion is a positive one, but in this case we are fully aware of the changing and transient nature of the universe. We can see the wolf at our heels, and we know that we must move on. Here, though, the journeyer may pause briefly in the warmth and light of the sun, absorbing and applying its energy to the work ahead. This time we won't need to be blasted out of our safe position, but will rather choose to leave it in order to continue on the journey.

SIGEL: sun

Phonetic equivalent: s

Tiw is a guiding star; well does it keep faith with princes;
it is ever on its course over the mists of night and never fails

Tyr or Tiw

Just as the second aett began with the cleansing destruction of haegl, so too does the third aett begin with a loss. However, hail is imposed by the Gods to force the sacrifice of those things which aren't really vital to our development. Tiw, on the other hand, represents a voluntary sacrifice, made by someone who understands exactly what they are giving up and why.

Tyr's sacrifice of his hand to allow the binding of the Fenris Wolf was a noble one, and notable in a pantheon of deities not known for their sense of duty and ethical responsibility. He is believed to be one of the oldest of the Norse Gods - a Bronze-age rock carving was found in Scandinavia depicting a one-handed warrior - and his position may well have originally superseded Odin. Tyr's rune is also one of the oldest in the futhark, having survived virtually unchanged from the earliest Bronze-age carvings.

It represents all those qualities associated with the God: strength, heroism, duty and responsibility. But it also represents a deeper mystery - that of the wounded God. Like thorn, the pain of Tiw focuses the attention and forces discipline. However, in this case the effect is more conscious and the wound carries a greater significance. Ur has been confronted and bound, and the lessons of Tiw and haegl have been learned. This is the path of the warrior.

The Anglo-Saxon rune poem connects the ancient god with the Pole Star, providing guidance through an ever-changing world. This constancy is in some ways the opposite of Eohl. Where Eohl is self-protection by setting up barriers, Tiw is the act of taking the fight.

TYR: Tyr, Tiw

Phonetic equivalent: t

The birch bears no fruit; yet without seed it brings forth suckers,

for it is generated from its leaves.

Splendid are its branches and gloriously adorned

its lofty crown which reaches to the skies.

Beorc

The birch is fundamentally a symbol of fertility. There are numerous instances in European folk tradition where birch twigs are to bring prosperity and encourage conception. They were fixed above a sweetheart's door on May Day in Cheshire, England, and were placed in stables and houses to promote fertility. On the continent, young men, women and cattle were struck with birch twigs for this same purpose, and young boys would be sent out to "beat the bounds of the parish" with branches of birch to prosperity in the coming year. Witches were said to ride broomsticks made from birch, an image which probably originated with fertility rituals where dancers would 'ride' brooms through the fields, the height of their jumping indicating how high the grain should grow.

If Tyr is the fundamental male mystery, then beorc certainly belongs to the women, for it represents the path of the mother, the healer and the midwife, bringing new life after death just as the birch puts out the first leaves after winter. While Tyr's wound is acquired through his encounter with death, beorc's wound is that of menstruation, and her ordeal is that of childbirth. The birch is abundant and all providing, and heals through nourishment, cleansing and empathy.

BEORC: birch

Phonetic equivalent: b

The horse is a joy to princes in the presence of warriors.
A steed in the pride of its hoofs,
when rich men on horseback bandy words about it;
and it is ever a source of comfort to the restless.

Eh

The horse has been a powerful symbol in nearly every culture and every age. They were often believed to draw the sun about heavens. Strong, swift and loyal, their relationship with humankind is unique. They allow us to perform tasks that would normally be beyond our strength, and to travel distances that would normally be beyond our reach. The mare symbolizes fertility fecundity, and the stallion is the epitome of virility and raw energy. It is an animal that never lost its power by being domesticated.

Like the sun which is its counterpart, eh represents energy and motion. In this case, however, there is also respect for the source of the power to be considered. This is not merely an impersonal energy source - it is a living, breathing thing whose needs and desires must be taken into consideration, rather than be simply used as a slave. This is the power that was given by the God at os, and this rune reminds us of our oath to only use it to help, never to harm. Like the two-edged sword, the horse is a powerful tool, but must be carefully controlled to avoid harming yourself or other. It is tempting to just go barrelling along recklessly, but to do so is to risk losing that power forever. This is the balance that must be achieved on the path of pure magic.

EH: horse

Phonetic equivalent: e (as in "egg")

The joyous man is dear to his kinsmen;
yet every man is doomed to fail his fellow,
since the Lord by his decree will commit the vile carrion to the earth.

Man

In its broadest sense, man represents all of humanity, and therefore the entire realm of Middle Earth. In more practical terms, it is those with whom we have personal connections, from our immediate circle of family and friends to the wider community around us, reminding us of our nature as social animals. It also represents our connection with the Gods (Ymir), and with nature (the two trees). It takes the raw energy of eh and controls it through our social conscience, reminding us of those we affect with our deeds both magical and mundane.

There is a warning with this rune, however. The second and third lines convey a very strong idea common through Anglo-Saxon and Mediaeval literature that life is fleeting. Death comes in many forms and it is the one thing that can be guaranteed. This rune reminds us that over-reliance on those around us can lead to problems.

MAN: mankind

Phonetic equivalent: m

The ocean seems interminable to men,
if they venture on the rolling bark
and the waves of the sea terrify them
and the courser of the deep heed not its bridle.

Lagu

When most people think of water, they generally thinkof its more pleasant associations - peacefulness, love, compassion, intuition, and the emotions in general. However, we must remember that, to the Norse, water most often meant the sea, and the sea was a terrifying, unpredictable place, home of the Midgard serpent and the grave of many sailors. Lagu, then, should be thought of in terms of the lighter and the darker sides of the element of water. It speaks to our primal fears of the dark, the cold, and all those terrifying things hidden deep within our subconscious minds.

This is a rune that takes the fatality of peorth and controls it. The important word in the poem is 'seems'. A good seaman will read the patterns of the ocean and trim his ship accordingly.

LAGU: water

Phonetic equivalent: l

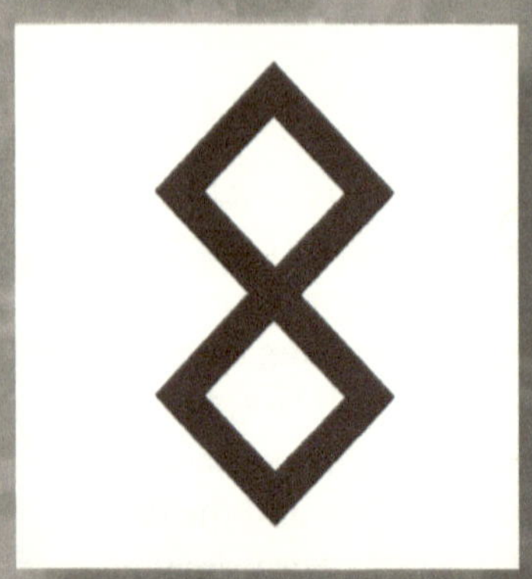

Ing was first seen by men among the East-Danes,
till, followed by his chariot,
he departed eastwards over the waves.
So the Heardingas named the hero.

Ing

Ing is a Danish/Anglo-Saxon name for Freyr, the God of agriculture and fertility. Agriculture represents one of the first attempts by mankind to control the environment, and the fertility of crops, animals and people has always been the primary concern and religious focus of most Pagan agrarian societies. From the earliest Sumerian accounts to modern-day British folk custom, people throughout history have sought to ensure the success of their crops.

The vast majority of people in Western society have lost all contact and connection with the land and the process of growing things. The spiritual consequences of this segregation from the earth have been disastrous, since most people find it difficult to relate to deity in a purely man-made environment. The shape of this rune can be likened to that of a field, but its real significance may lie in its balance, representing the harmonious relationship between ourselves and the four elements/four directions. Ing reminds us of that ancient connection between the Gods and the land, and re-links us with our spiritual natures through the realm of the physical. It is quite literally a grounding rune, and by reintroducing us to the earth, it reconnects our bodies, our minds and our spirits.

ING: ing

Phonetic equivalent: ng

An estate is very dear to every man,

if he can enjoy there in his house

whatever is right and proper in constant prosperity

Othel

In othel, we find ourselves back in the seemingly mundane realm of wealth and property, just like the first rune, fehu. However, while cattle represented a more movable, transitory form of wealth, the land is the only thing thatlasts. It can be passed on as a legacy, but more importantly, it defines who we are by defining where we are. It is, ultimately, our home.

This rune brings us to the seventh cardinal point, which is the centre. It is the meeting place between Midgaard and Asgard; between ourselves and our Gods. It is the axis around which our lives revolve. The idea of land or property is only a symbol - we must all find our own "centre" (or, as Joseph Campbell termed it, our "bliss") to give our lives meaning, and this is really the ultimate goal of the runic journey. Like Dorothy in the Wizard of Oz, we discoverthat after all our travels and adventures, we all eventually end up going home. But this doesn't mean that the travels and adventures are pointless. On the contrary, it is only through those explorations that our 'home' or spiritual centre can have any real meaning for us. "There's no place like home" of will have no power to send us there unless we come to truly understand what and where our home is to us. Conversely, none of lessons learned along the way can be of any real use to us unless we actively integrate them into our 'mundane' lives and find that centre point to anchor them to.

OTHEL: property, home

Phonetic equivalent: o

Day, the glorious light of the Creator, is sent by the Lord;

it is beloved of men, a source of hope and happiness to rich and poor,

and of service to all

Daeg

This rune effectively marks the end of the third aett. As in the previous two aetts, daeg concludes the third with light and hope. However, while wynn represented earthly glories and sigel the sun, heavenly the day brings these two realms together, bringing the more abstract light and power of sigel 'down to earth' and applying it to our everyday lives.

This is the joy of completion, of finally being able to sit back and rest after effort.

DAEG: day

Phonetic equivalent: d

The Wanderer

Often the lonely receives love,
The Creator's help, though heavy with care
Over the sea he suffers long
Stirring his hands in the frosty swell,
The way of exile. Wyrd never wavers.

The wanderer spoke; he told his sorrows,
The deadly onslaughts, the death of the clan,
"At dawn alone I must
Mouth my cares; the man does not live
Whom I dare tell my depths
Straight out. I see truth
In the lordly custom for the courageous man
To bind fast his breast, loyal
To his treasure closet, thoughts aside.
The weary cannot control wyrd
Nor do bitter thoughts settle things.
The eager for glory often bind
Something bloody close to their breasts.

"Wretched, I tie my heart with ropes
Far from my home, far from my kinsmen
Since a hole in the ground hid my chief
Long ago. Laden with cares,
Weary, I crossed the confine of waves,
Sought the troop of a dispenser of treasure,
Far or near to find the man
Who knew my merits in the mead hall,
Who would foster a friendless man,
Treat me to joys. He who has put it to a test
Knows how cruel a companion is sorrow
For one who has few friendly protectors.
Exile guards him, not wrought gold,
A freezing heart, not the fullness of the earth.

He remembers warriors, the hall, rewards,
How, as a youth, his friend honored him at feasts,
The gold-giving prince. Joy has perished,

"He knows how it is to suffer long
Without the beloved wisdom of a friendly lord.
Often when sorrow and sleep together
Bind the worn lonely warrior
It seems in his heart that he holds and kisses
The lord of the troop and lays on his knee
His head and hands as he had before
In times gone by at the gift-giver's throne.
When the friendless warrior awakens again
He sees before him the black waves,
Sea birds bathing, feathers spreading,
Frost and snow falling with hail.
The wounds of his heart are heavier,
Sore after his friends. Sorrow is renewed
When the mind ponders the memory of kinsmen;
He greets them with joy; he anxiously grasps
For something to say. They swim away again.
The breasts of ghosts do not bring the living
Much wisdom. Woe is renewed
For him who must send his weary heart
Way out over the prison of waves.

"Therefore in this world I cannot think of a reason
Why my soul does not blacken when I seriously consider
All the warriors, tested at war,
How they suddenly sank to the floor,
The brave kinsmen. But this world
Every day falls to dust.
No man is wise until he lives many winters
In the kingdom of the world.
The wise must be patient,

Never too hasty with feelings nor too hot with words
Nor too weak as a warrior nor too witlessly brash
Nor too fearful nor too ready nor too greedy for reward
Nor even too feverish for boasting until testing his fibre.
A man should wait before he makes a vow
Until, like a true warrior, he eagerly tests
Which way the courage of his heart will course.
The good warrior must understand how ghostly it will be
When all this world of wealth stands wasted
As now in many places about this massive earth
Walls stand battered by the wind,
Covered by frost, the roofs collapsed.
The wine halls crumbled; the warriors lie dead,
Cut off from joy; the great troop all crumpled
Proud by the wall. One war took,
Led to his death. One a bird lifted
Over the high sea. One the hoary wolf
Broke with death. One, bloody-cheeked,
A warrior hid in a hole in the ground.
Likewise God destroyed this earthly dwelling
Until the strongholds of the giants stood empty,
Without the sounds of joy of the city-dwellers."

Then the wise man thinks about the wall
And deeply considers this dark life.
From times far away the wanderer recalls
The deadly slashes and says,
"What happened to the horse?
What happened to the warrior?
What happened to the gift-giver?
What happened to the wine hall?
Where are the sounds of joy?
Ea-la bright beaker! Ea-la byrnied warrior!
Ea-la the chiefs majesty!
How those moments went,

Grayed in the night as if they never were!
A wall still stands near the tracks of the warriors,
Wondrously high! Worms have stained it.
A host of spears hungry for carnage
Destroyed the men, that marvelous wyrd!
Storms beat these stone cliffs,
A blanket of frost binds the earth,
Winter is moaning! When the mists darken
And night descends, the north delivers
A fury of hail in hatred at men.
All is wretched in the realm of the earth;
The way of wyrd changes the world under heaven.
Here is treasure lent, here is a friend lent,
Here is a man lent, here is a kinsman lent.
All of the earth will be empty!"

So spoke the wise in heart; he sits alone with his mystery.
He is good to keep faith; grief must never escape
A man's heart too quickly unless with his might like a true
warrior
He has sought a lasting boon. It is best for him who seeks
love,
Help from the heavenly Father where all stands firm.

Index of Runes